This delightful book is the latest in the series of Ladybird books which have been specially planned to help grown-ups with the world about them.

As in the other books in this series, the large clear script, the careful choice of words, the frequent repetition and the thoughtful matching of text with pictures all enable grown-ups to think they have taught themselves to cope. The subject of the book will greatly appeal to grown-ups.

Series 999

THE LADYBIRD
BOOKS FOR GROWN—UPS SERIES

THE PEOPLE NEXT DOOR

by

J.A. HAZELEY, N.S.F.W. and J.P. MORRIS, O.M.G.

(Authors of 'Drawing On The Right Side Of The Paper')

Publishers: Ladybird Books Ltd., Loughborough
Printed in England. If wet, Italy.

Our planet is small and we must learn to share with each other.

Every Sunday, at dawn, Neil sits outside his house, sharing the deafening engine noise of his unmuffled vintage M.G. roadster with the rest of the street who are having a lie-in.

Not everything needs sharing.

The houses on this new estate may all look the same, but the people who are moving in have big ideas.

Tom and Susy are planning to fill their garden with purple and white flowers.

Mickey and Sylvia have their hearts set on a selection of mattresses and motorcycle parts.

Every dream home is different.

Logan is reporting his next—door neighbour to the police again.

This time, it's for using a hairdryer before 8am. Last time, it was for trespass by blossom.

"You again," says the duty sergeant, and gets the forms.

Nobody on Twebbin Way knows anything about the Routledges.

The people opposite once saw Mr Routledge receive a delivery of hovercraft parts, and there are rumours that the children, who are home—schooled, only eat mushrooms.

There may also be more than one Mrs Routledge.

Mina planted some genetically modified asparagus seeds in her vegetable patch before she went on a two-week holiday.

When she comes home, she finds a note from the couple next door saying they would like a word.

Chloe and Harry are convinced that Mr Benbecula is up to something.

After six months, Nat stopped believing the constant drilling from next door could be shelves.

He now thinks it is either a transatlantic tunnel, fracking, or an attempt to find a lost dinosaur kingdom at the earth's core.

He would pop round and ask them, but next door cannot hear their doorbell over the drill.

"These handsome flats were buil
as social housing for ordinary
working people," it says in the
expensive architecture books or
the coffee tables of the doctors
creatives and architects who live
in them now.

The people who live below Lisa and Marc are environmentalists.

Because they always leave their windows open, the environment constantly benefits from their aggressive chill-out music and the smell of their unusual cigarettes

Petuwaq and Aqpalibaaqtuq are
building a new igloo.

The people next door are not
pleased.

"Look at that monstrosity," they
say. "Ah, well. There goes the
neighbourhood."

Vicky's upstairs neighbour is always crying. He plays the song "Rise" by Gabrielle five or six times an hour.

Vicky thinks he either misses his wife or his job in local radio in the early 2000s.

Ever since the ESA capsule docked, Bruno has been sharing the International Space Station with an astronaut who insists on being called The Jonester.

The Jonester has made the joke "Need some space, man?" every two minutes since arriving.

Bruno wishes the International Space Station had a predatory alien on board that picked the astronauts off one by one. He wouldn't mind in which order.

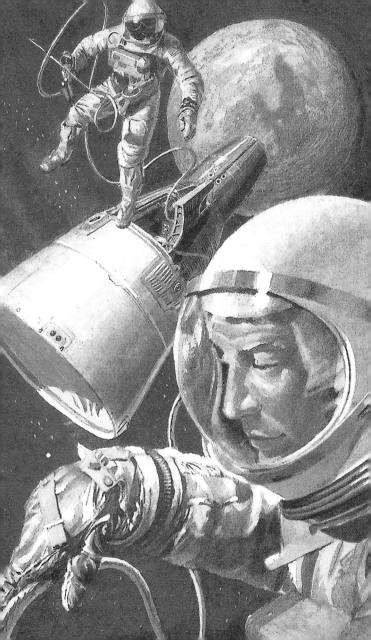

Before the financial crash, Troy lived in the apartment next door to David Letterman.

Now he lives in the shack next door to One-Eyed Pete and his silent son.

Troy never talks about his old job to Pete, because it was his bank who repossessed Pete's old flat and made him sell the eye.

Craig thought his neon Father Christmas and singing snowman were going to be the talk of The Close but he has to admit the Khaings at number 15 have pulled out all the stops this year.

Stephen and Jon have lived in their flat for ten years.

In the first year, a pregnant couple moved in next door. Their baby kept Stephen and Jon awake for two years, before the family moved on to a bigger flat.

They were replaced by another pregnant couple no fewer than five times.

Stephen and Jon are more tired than any of the people they have lived next door to.

Sharon has asked the man next door if he would mind not parking his company car in front of her house.

She is worried about her cat.

A hungry dolphin can make an awful lot of noise.

Lucy wishes she had done more than skim-read the planning application when her neighbour mentioned putting in a water feature.

Trevor became so tired of his neighbour's bassoon practice that he decided to move to somewhere far from other people.

Going to the shops for a pint of milk requires permission from Air Traffic Control, but Trevor says it is worth it to live free from persistent bassooning.

Nick swapped his headboard to the other wall yesterday and now knows exactly what Paul's wife wants him to do of an evening and just how hard.

Nick avoids making eye contact and asks Paul about trowels.

Russell shows his sister Denise the device he has made from his electronics kit.

When he presses the button, it completes the circuit and summons the ghost of the boy next door.

Spartacus next door has a new tree—house. Now Shauna and Dylan will want one too.

First it was a Swingball set, then it was a trampoline.

Shauna and Dylan's mum knows she must put her foot down before it's skis, a hot tub and the Gardenstock Grime Festival.

Rachel and Robert's neighbour Mrs Vavasour has complained to the council about their hedge, their cat and the colour of their front door.

The morning after Rachel left her hair straighteners plugged in, Mrs Vavasour complains to the council that she was kept awake by a bright, flickering orange light and the sound of exploding wood.

Rebecca ordered a farmer from a speciality website, but she was out when the courier called.

The delivery has been left in next door's porch, as arranged.

Since Lauren and her husband separated, her children have started to play with the children next door.

Lauren's husband did not like the people next door.

"They're ginger," he used to say. "It's not right."

THE AUTHORS would like to record their gratitude and offer their apologies to the many Ladybird artists whose luminous work formed the glorious wallpaper of countless childhoods. Revisiting it for this book as grown-ups has been a privilege.

MICHAEL JOSEPH

UK | USA | Canada | Ireland | Australia
India | New Zealand | South Africa

Michael Joseph is part of the Penguin Random House group of companies whose addresses can be found at global.penguinrandomhouse.com

First published 2016
001

Copyright © Jason Hazeley and Joel Morris, 2016
All images copyright © Ladybird Books Ltd, 2016

The moral right of the authors has been asserted

Printed in Italy by L.E.G.O. S.p.A

A CIP catalogue record for this book is available from the British Library

ISBN: 978–0–718–18441–4

www.greenpenguin.co.uk

Penguin Random House is committed to a sustainable future for our business, our readers and our planet. This book is made from Forest Stewardship Council® certified paper.